Books by Christine Thomas Doran

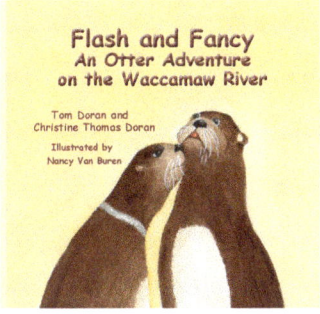

Flash and Fancy
An Otter Adventure
on the Waccamaw River

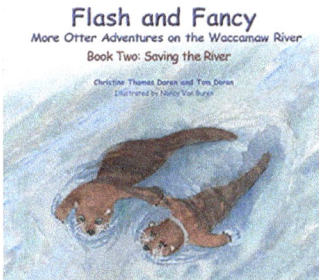

Flash and Fancy
More Otter Adventure
on the Waccamaw River

**Tabby Kittens
at Midnight**

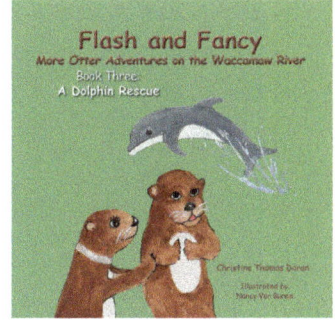

Flash and Fancy
More Otter Adventure
on the Waccamaw River
A Dolphin Rescue

Maddie's Choice

Christine Thomas Doran

Maddie's Choice
Copyright © 2019
Chrisine Thomas Doran

All rights reserved.
This publication may not be reproduced, stored in a retrieval system, or transmitted in any form, recording, mechanical, electronic, or photocopy, without written permission of the author. The only exception is brief quotations used in book reviews.

Comments:
flashandfancy@gmail.com

Illustrations by
Nancy Van Buren

ISBN:
Paper back 978-1-941069-98-1
Hard cover 978-1-9411069-99-8

Published by Prose Press
Pawleys Island, SC 29585
proseNcons@live.com

WingMan Books, is a division of
Addiction Resource Systems, Inc..
Dedicated to educating
children of all ages about the hazards of
addiction and addictive behavior.

addictionresourcesystems.com

zaddiction.com/

*Children, our most valuable resource;
may they all be Dragonslayers!*

Acknowledgments

Thank you, Bob O'Brien. You are the inspiration for this writing project; your encouragement and enthusiasm in using the Wingman and the dragon concept helped to bring the characters to life with this crucial message.

A special thank you to my sister, Nita Brady, for the allegorical approach of the dragonslayer. Your creativity allowed me to incorporate it into my story! Thanks for all the encouragement that was offered during this project that addresses such an extremely important topic in today's society.

MADDIE'S CHOICE

"Ahhh…this is the life!" said ten-year-old Maddie. She stretched and settled into her cozy, bright pink bean bag nest-of-a chair. In her lap, she cradled a new fantasy book like a precious puppy. Maddie loved reading about magical fairies, courageous knights, and ferocious dragons—her favorite genre!

The quietness of her special reading place surrounded Maddie like a soft downy comforter. An unused closet in the front hallway had been fashioned into a cozy nook by her creative mother. Painted her favorite bright pink, she had placed some of her prized possessions into her reading place—a fluffy, pink rug adorned the floor, and the bean bag chair sat upon it like a fairy queen's throne. Next to it stood a pink floor lamp, its pink shade sprinkled with white polka dots. Against a wall there was a small bookcase that she and her mom had painted a pale pink, of course! Its shelves held Maddie's favorite books and fairy figurines. Decorating the walls were posters of fairies with translucent wings dressed in filmy, gauzy dresses in an explosion of every color of the rainbow.

Fairies held a fascination for Maddie, and she thought of them as her special friends. One fairy in particular, Fleury, was a very special secret friend. Fleury was like her guardian angel, and Maddie often felt her presence. Fleury had dark brown hair and dark eyes. She wore a tiny, dark pink tutu, and her translucent wings shimmered with purple, pink, and green iridescence. On this particular Saturday afternoon, Maddie was so into her book that she didn't hear the cell phone chiming melodically from down the hallway. The spell was broken when her mother's voice called out to her.

"Maddie!" her mom called loudly. "Maddie, you've got a phone call!"

"Oh! Okay, mom! Coming!" she called back. Maddie was in an exciting part of the book, and she didn't want to stop reading. Reluctantly, she put a bookmark between the pages marking her place.

Maddie rushed down the hallway to the sewing room that was her mom's favorite place. The comforting, humming sound of the sewing machine greeted her as she entered the cheerful room. She wondered who could be calling her.

"Hello," Maddie spoke into her mom's cell phone that she secretly wished was her own.

The familiar voice of her best friend answered her back, "Hi, Maddie. This is Emma. What're you doing?" her friend asked. Emma had been her best friend since first grade, and they had spent a lot of time together. Lately, though, she hadn't seen much of her friend. Emma always seemed to be busy when she had called her.

"Oh, hi Emma! I was reading. What're you up to?" Maddie asked. It was good to hear her friend's voice.

Emma said, "Oh, Maddie! I'm over at Olivia's house, and we're having a way awesome time! It's more fun than sitting around reading a book on a Saturday afternoon!" Maddie could hear the laughter in Emma's voice, and she realized that she wanted to be over there, too.

Olivia was a neighbor girl who was a thirteen-year-old middle schooler. She was very pretty and popular, and both Maddie and Emma admired and looked up to her. They thought Olivia was just the coolest girl ever because of her long beautiful dark hair and the stylish clothes she wore. So, when Emma invited her to go over to the older girl's house, she jumped at the chance.

Maddie exclaimed, "Wow! Okay! Let me ask my mom!" She turned to her mom, flashed her brightest smile, and explained, "Mom, Emma's over at Olivia's house, and they want me to come over. Please, please may I go?"

Sensing her eagerness, mom agreed, "Well, okay,

but just be home by 5:00 for dinner. We're having your favorite—spaghetti, garlic bread, and salad."

"Oh thanks, mom!" said Maddie. Her green eyes sparkled with excitement as she got back on the phone with her friend. "Emma, my mom said okay! I'll be there in a flash!" With a quick kiss and a warm hug, she said goodbye to her mom.

Maddie quickly made a dash to the front door. She hopped down the two front steps and skipped over to where her shiny magenta painted bike was parked. A nearby azalea shrub burst forth with beautiful pink blossoms.

The radiance of the flowers matched the color of Maddie's cheeks and the exuberance she was feeling. She jumped on her bike and pedaled furiously down the street full speed ahead. Her long, shiny red ringlets flowed out behind her in the gentle breeze like a fluffy red cloud.

Maddie soon arrived at the lovely brick home where Olivia lived. She bounded up the front steps as swiftly as a young gazelle. Before she could even knock, the front door swung open, and her two friends greeted her with huge grins.

"Well, well, look who's here," blond-haired Emma teased with a twinkle in her eyes. "How's the little bookworm?"

"Oh, I'm good!" answered Maddie, as she and Emma followed Olivia into her spacious family room.

Turning around to face the two younger girls, Olivia looked directly at Maddie and Emma. She paused before asking in a mischievous and secretive voice, "Hey, you two want to have a little fun?"

"What kind of fun?" responded a curious Maddie. She wondered why Olivia sounded so sneaky.

"Oh, I know," giggled Emma. She and Olivia exchanged glances like they were sharing a secret. All at once, they both burst into laughter.

Twirling a lock of dark hair with her finger, Olivia looked at Maddie and patted the sofa with her other hand. She said, "Now Maddie, I want you to sit right here on the sofa and close your eyes. I have a surprise for you." She and Emma started to giggle again.

Feeling a little excited, Maddie did as she was told. What was Olivia was up to? The squeaky sound of a cabinet door could be heard opening and closing.

"No peeking!" Emma playfully laughed.

The delicate clinking of glasses on the marble top coffee table aroused Maddie's curiosity even more. She wondered what kind of game this was. It suddenly occurred to her that the rest of the house was very quiet, and she also wondered if Olivia's parents were at home.

"Okay, Maddie! You can open your eyes now! Ta-da!" Olivia exclaimed. She said this with importance, as if she had just won a small victory.

To Maddie's delight, a pretty chocolate-brown bottle sat gleaming before her eyes. Next to it, Olivia had set out three small matching crystal glasses. Into the glasses, the middle schooler poured a creamy pale-brown liquid that almost looked like chocolate milk.

"Wow! Is this some kind of party?" Maddie asked in awe.

Spreading her arms in front of the crystal display, Olivia explained, "Oh, this is the fun I was telling you about, Maddie. See, it says Irish Cream on the label. It'll make you feel all warm and fuzzy all the way down to your toes and make you feel sooo relaxed!" Maddie wondered if Olivia had already sampled this drink because of the silly way her voice sounded.

"Hmmm," hesitated Maddie. "What exactly is it again?" she put the small crystal glass up to her little freckled nose. A delicious aroma whirled into her senses like a steaming cup of hot chocolate on a winter's day.

Emma stated knowingly, "It's whiskey, and it makes you feel exactly like the way Olivia said it would. I had some the other day, and I felt as if I were floating on a cloud. It's fun, Maddie! C'mon! Try some!" Emma took a sip and smacked her lips and said with pleasure, "Yummy!"

Then, Olivia did the same thing, except that she took a big gulp instead of a little sip. "Wow! I love that rush of warmth all the way down to my tippy toes! Mmmm," she said as she flopped down on the sofa next to Maddie and Emma. Maddie wondered again where Olivia's parents were. "Maddie, I know you secretly want to take a sip," she whispered playfully into the younger girl's ear.

"Olivia, where're your parents?" Maddie quietly asked.

Rolling her eyes, Olivia murmured casually, "Oh, they aren't here right now. They went out of town and won't be back till late tonight. Oh, Maddie! Don't look so gloomy… c'mon…chill."

"Oh," Maddie replied in a dull voice. "Well, I was just wondering." She was beginning to feel very uncomfortable. Although Maddie was only a child, she knew that this whiskey was a kind of alcohol, even if it smelled like a warm chocolate brownie.

A recent discussion with her parents had made Maddie very aware of whiskey. The conversation had been about her dad's brother, her Uncle Tony. They had told her that Uncle Tony had a bad alcohol problem and that he especially loved to drink whiskey. Her dad had sadly explained that drinking alcohol had ruined his life. Uncle Tony had lost his job, his house, and then finally he'd lost his family. He was now homeless! Yes, Maddie had heard of whiskey, maybe not Irish Cream Whiskey that smelled and looked so chocolaty, and she knew it was very, very bad for you. The uncle that she loved so much was now an alcoholic because of drinking so much.

Emma continued to pressure her, "C'mon, Maddie. Take just one teeny weeny taste. You're going to love it!" She and Olivia each took their last sip of whiskey. Then, the young teenager stood up and refilled their little glasses, and the sipping continued. Maddie's glass remained untouched.

Maddie was beginning to feel like she didn't even know these girls anymore. Olivia and Emma burst into a fit of laughter, and she began to worry that her friends were getting drunk. She couldn't believe how goofy they were acting as they pirouetted around the room.

Maddie just sat quietly on the sofa and stared at the exquisite little glasses of chocolaty creamy liquid. How could something that looked and smelled so good be so bad for you? But, she knew it was true. Looking up from the sofa, she stared at them right into their eyes. Maddie stated firmly, "You know, I'm good. I don't think so."

"Oh, c'mon Maddie! All the cool and popular kids drink! Trust me! We have some beer, too!" gushed her older friend. Her eyes were shining brightly as she went over to the computer and turned on some rock music full blast.

Maddie stood up and almost had to yell, "No way! My parents would ground me for life if they ever found out I drank alcohol!" She watched the two girls dance wildly around the room. Once again, Maddie felt like her friends were now strangers...like she didn't know who they were.

"Woo-hoo! No parents! Partaaay!" yelled Olivia above the blaring music.

Suddenly, Maddie heard a little whisper in her ear, and she recognized the magical, musical voice to be that of her tiny fairy friend, Fleury. "Psst! Maddie," said the dazzling

fairy. "Real friends would never want you to do anything that would harm or hurt you! Olivia and Emma aren't your friends, I'm sorry to say. What they want you to do is dangerous and could even kill you! Alcohol and drugs can ruin your hopes and dreams for your future. Choose life, Maddie, and not the lies." Maddie already knew this, but the soothing words of Fleury brought her great comfort and a feeling of peace within herself.

Maddie stated with more emphasis, "Well, I can be cool without drinking! It's not for me, and I know for a fact it's very bad to drink alcohol!"

Again, the still small voice of Fleury whispered in Maddie's ear. She was like a miniature coach, encouraging her on,

"Good job, Maddie! Remember to always stay true to who you are!"

Abruptly, Maddie got up from the sofa. She stated firmly, "I'm going home! Anyway, what's it to you whether I drink alcohol or not?" Her heart was pounding in her chest and her hands were shaking. Fighting back tears, she sadly turned away from the two girls who had once stood beside her as friends. With a new confidence, Maddie made her way through the family room toward the front door. She heard Olivia's taunting voice behind her.

"Maddie, you are just so annoying and so uncool, you know that?" Olivia hissed. Her alcohol reminded Maddie of one of the terrible fire-breathing dragons in the fantasy books she loved to read. The evil creatures roamed around the villages terrorizing and destroying the lives of innocent people. Right then, Maddie made a promise to herself. She would never let the evil dragon of alcohol or drugs take away or destroy her future dreams and goals.

Her heart was still pounding as Maddie opened the

front door and ran down the porch steps. She turned around, faced her friends, and said strongly, "You know what? You two are the uncool ones. Real friends would never, ever want their friend to do something that would hurt or harm her. I choose life, not your lies!" Fleury's wise words still echoed in her ear. Bam! I just slayed that dragon! I'm like one of the dragonslayers I read about, she thought triumphantly!

Olivia laughed and shrugged her shoulders. She jeered, "Whatever! It's your choice if you want to be a total loser!" Emma just stood next to Olivia on the porch with her arms crossed in front of her chest. On her lips she wore a smug little smirk. This really hurts, Maddie thought as she again fought back the burning tears. Seeing Emma standing like that next to Olivia just made her heart hurt in her chest.

Maddie rushed toward her bike, hopped on, and pedaled furiously toward her house. "I don't need friends like that!" she said aloud. Then, out of nowhere, Maddie felt the soft flutter of Fleury's wings near her right shoulder. She heard the still small voice whisper into her ear, "Great job, Maddie! You made the smart choice not to let alcohol get in your way. I'm proud of you! You're a dragonslayer!" Fleury's promising words brought a smile to Maddie's cute sweet face.

"Thank you, my little guardian fairy friend," Maddie whispered into the fragrant afternoon air.

She glanced over her right shoulder back at Olivia's house. Maddie let out a deep sigh. It could have been such a great day, she thought with sadness. Her wish for Olivia and Emma was that they would become strong and be able to resist the deadly fire-breathing dragon of alcohol and drugs. It wasn't that she didn't like them anymore. More than anything, she was very worried about their behavior and attitude about drinking. Maddie wanted her friends to someday be able to achieve their future dreams and to grow up to be healthy and successful. She wanted them to be dragonslayers, too!

Riding her bike up the street where she lived, Maddie's white, two-story house soon came into view. She pedaled through the front yard, jumped off, and then parked her bike by the beautiful pink azalea shrub. A feeling of great sadness came over her, and she sighed deeply again. What should I do now, she struggled within herself. Should I tell mom about Emma and Olivia and all that had happened?

Maddie stood by the front door for a couple of minutes still trying to figure out the best thing to do. What should she say? She knew her mother would be wondering why she was home so early. All at once, the little girl knew what she absolutely must do. She HAD to tell her mom. The nearby presence of Fleury encouraged her to make that big decision.

"Thank you, Fleury," she whispered. "You're my true friend!"

Fleury giggled and winked at Maddie, and then with a flurry of her wings, she vanished into the warm breezy air.

Turning the doorknob slowly, Maddie took a deep

breath and entered into the bright front hallway of her comforting home.

THE END

WingMan Books are available at some local stores and all on-line outlets

CHILDREN'S

WingMan Chronicles 1 - Spike, Christine Medicus and Bob O'Brien

WingMan Chronicles 2 - WingMan, Christine Medicus and Bob O'Brien

Joyous Jayden, Christine Medicus

Billy the Bully, Pat David

PRE-TEENS/TEENS
Peer Mentoring

The Dragon Slayers Club, Nita Brady

Choose Life, Christine Thomas Doran

Am I Fixed, Pat David

Maddie's Choice, Christine Thomas Doran

ADULT

Witness, Lee W. Hollingsworth

Misinformed Hearts, (Screenplay), Beverley Gadarda

SCHOOLS and COUNSELORS

The Dragon Slayers Club, Nita Brady

WINGMAN
Break Free - Stay Free

WingMan Books, is a division of
Addiction Resource Systems, Inc..
Dedicated to educating
children of all ages about the hazards of
addiction and addictive behavior.
addictionresourcesystems.com
zaddiction.com/